I Sailed with Columbus

MIRIAM SCHLEIN

I Sailed with Columbus

Illustrated by Tom Newsom

A TRUMPET CLUB SPECIAL EDITION

Published by The Trumpet Club
666 Fifth Avenue, New York, New York 10103

Text copyright © 1991 by Miriam Schlein
Illustrations copyright © 1991 by Tom Newsom

ISBN 0-440-84873-3

This edition published by arrangement with
HarperCollins Children's Books, a division of
HarperCollins Publishers
Printed in the United States of America
September 1992

3 5 7 9 10 8 6 4 2
OPM

Contents

Some Names and Places

Cristóbal Colón: Columbus's name in Spanish. In Italy, where he was born, his name was Cristoforo Colombo. We know him as Columbus, which is the Latin form of the name.

The Indies: the name given in Columbus's day to the area of most of eastern Asia—China, Japan, India, and Myanmar (formerly called Burma).

Cipangu: the name for Japan at that time.

Cathay: the name for China at that time.

Quinsay: a great city in China at that time (now called Hangzhou).

Part I

The Voyage West

My name is Julio . . .

My name is Julio de la Vega Medina. I am
twelve and tall for my age. I row well. I can climb
like a monkey. And the Franciscan Brothers have
taught me to write. At first I thought it was for
this reason the ship's master took me on. After
all, in the Canary Islands where I come from,
most boys can climb and row. But not many can
write, and read, as I do. Later I found out there
was another reason. It was because I could sing!
Imagine! Here I am, on this great voyage, sailing
west on her majesty's ship *Santa María*, with the
great explorer Cristóbal Colón . . . all because I
can sing!

It is strange how things happen.

I started life as an orphan. My mother died
when I was born. My father died a month before,
in a storm at sea, when a whaling boat turned
over. But the Franciscan Brothers took me in and

brought me up. So it's not like I have no family. I have a large, wonderful family of fathers, brothers, uncles. They could not have been kinder to me. And it is not because I don't love them a lot that I am leaving them. It is because I have this chance to do something wonderful. How many boys get a chance like this?

One thing I did at the friary was help Brother Gustavo raise canaries. Of course there are wild canaries all over the Canary Islands. But the ones we raise are more yellow than the wild ones, and sing sweeter melodies. About once a month I would go to town, to San Sebastián, to sell some.

One day I had sold all but one, when a tall, blue-eyed man stopped to admire my bird. "Our birds are the best," I said proudly. I whistled a tune and showed him how the little bird could mimic it perfectly. He listened, smiled, and seemed almost about to buy it. But then he just shook his head and walked on.

When I finally sold the last bird, I walked down to the harbor. There was a feeling of excitement down there—more than usual. There were three ships in the harbor—three big ones at once. This was unusual, too. There seemed to be a great hurry to get them loaded.

I stood watching. "Hey, you. Do you want to earn a few maravedies?"

I looked. The man in charge was talking to me. Before I knew it, I was helping with the loading. There was another boy around my age. His name was Luis. We worked together, carrying on barrels of salted sardines and anchovies . . . pickled beef . . . cheeses and kegs of molasses. Casks of wine.

As we worked, we sang and talked—that is, when we had the breath for singing and talking. Luis was from Seville. He had signed on as a gromet—a ship's boy. I could see the voyage was going to be a long one. Just look at how many casks of water they were carrying on board!

I asked Luis: Had he ever sailed before?

"No."

And why was he going now?

"Because I will come back a rich man! Think of how easy life will be for my mother when I come back with pockets full of gold . . . and maybe some rubies!"

"Rubies? Where are these ships going?"

"Where?" My new friend stopped short so suddenly, we nearly dropped the big cheese between us. He seemed astonished at my ignorance. "Have you not heard? These are the vessels of Queen Isabella and King Ferdinand of Spain. We are sailing west to the Indies. To Cipangu. And then to Cathay." Luis whispered, "Did you know, in Cathay the roofs are made of gold? I thought everybody heard about this voyage!"

I didn't hear much news. I didn't come down very often from the friary. None of the Franciscan Brothers do. I had not heard this news. But something special *was* going on. I couldn't help but notice. There were mules loaded with strange goods. One carried sacks filled with hundreds of little bells—the kind you put on hawks. Who would need so many hawk bells?

I did know one thing: You do not sail *west* to the Indies. To get to the Indies, you sail *east*, through the Mediterranean. Then travel overland, across Asia. Or, a vessel could sail south, around the tip of Africa, then east. But never *west*. I wondered whether Luis was mistaken.

I soon learned that Luis knew what he was

talking about. It was when Captain Vincente Pinzón himself came up to me. (I did not know who he was at the time.) I had noticed him watching me. Especially when Luis and I began to sing. And he was surprised when he dropped a bit of paper, and I picked it up and said, "Here's your list of supplies, Sir."

"How do you know what it is?"

"I can read it," I said. He shook his head. Luis and I went on with our work.

It was soon after that that he asked me if I wanted to sign up as a gromet on the *Santa María*, for five hundred maravedies a month. He explained that one of the boys had gotten sick, and could not sail. They were sailing the very next day. He told me it was a voyage that no one had ever made before—traveling west to the Indies—and that we would see things no one had ever seen before. He added, smiling, that I would come back a rich and happy boy.

Rich? Happy? I was already happy. I had never wanted for anything. Why did I need gold? But to do something no one has ever done before . . . see sights no one has ever seen. That's the idea that excited me.

I told him I would have to talk to the Brothers about it. He told me if I wanted to go, I would have to be back early the next day.

I walked back to the friary fast, in a daze. I even forgot to get the twenty-five maravedies I had earned for my help in the loading.

That night, all the Brothers helped me decide.

"Think of all you can learn," they said. "And all you will see. . . ."

In the end, we all decided my answer should be yes.

At dawn Brother Ernesto (he who had spent long hours helping me learn to read and write) and Brother Gustavo (he whom I helped to breed the canaries) walked back with me to town, helping me carry my few possessions. They made arrangements with Captain Pinzón. Part of my earnings were to be paid out to them now to keep for me. Part I was to receive on my return. The agreement was dated Thursday, 6 September 1492.

I embraced Ernesto and Gustavo one last time. Then I boarded the flagship *Santa María*. It was not a moment too soon. In half an hour we weighed anchor. And shortly before noon we set sail. As we left the harbor, I looked back. The last

8

thing I saw were two gray specks, still standing on the dock. The two friars I loved the best. Would I ever see them again? Was I doing the right thing? It was too late to worry about it now.

The Santa Maria | **6 September 1492. Day 1.** Since I had no duties as yet, I looked around. The *Santa Maria* is big. I judged it to be seventy feet at least. (I learned later it is seventy-seven feet.) The deck is painted red. The raised bulwarks are shiny black. Everything is newly painted and shipshape. I noticed something else. There are bombardas (swivel guns) mounted on the side-rails. I have heard, of course, of pirates that attack ships at sea. Will we have to defend ourselves? My life with the Brothers has been so peaceful. I know nothing about guns, and little about fighting.

The *Santa Maria* has three masts. On the big square mainsail is the royal insignia showing a lion and a castle. As we left the harbor, the *Santa Maria* sailed first. Close behind came the *Niña* and the *Pinta*. It was only fitting that we led the way, since the *Santa Maria* is the flagship that carries the Captain General himself, Cristóbal Colón.

But once in the open sea, the other two vessels tacked to the starboard and quickly overtook us. Not only did they pass us, but in doing so, they blocked our wind, causing our sails to go limp. As the others sailed merrily by, the *Niña* was closest. We could see their captain giving a salute.

A man came down from our poop deck (a raised section at the stern), pausing for a moment to stare up at our drooping sails. "By San Fernando, this thing is a tub!" He thumped the bulwark with the flat of his hand. He strode down the deck. "They will reach the Indies before us. . . ."

I stared after him. He was tall. Silver haired. Blue eyes, dimple in the chin. I knew him. He was the man who nearly bought my last canary!

Just then Luis appeared at my side. "The Captain General is not happy with our ship. He keeps calling it a tub. But we'll do fine. We're the biggest!"

"That man," I said, "is the Captain General? That is Cristóbal Colón?"

I thought back to how I had whistled and chatted and boasted to him, the Captain General! I felt like a fool. But how could I know who he was?

"You can help me," Luis said, breaking into my thoughts.

At last I could do something useful. We raised the hatch. Luis climbed below deck. I followed. Together we carried up biscuits, fruit, and wine, which we handed out to the seamen.

Our course was set due west. Once the fleet spread out a bit, and our wind was not "stolen," the *Santa María* kept up well with the others. As the sun sank lower, we headed straight for it. The wind was behind us. The sea was gentle.

At sunset a gromet lighted the binnacle lamp at the stern. Then all hands gathered on deck for evening prayers.

Together the raggle-taggle crew, heads bowed, hands folded, recited the Lord's Prayer. "Our Father who art in heaven, Hallowed be thy name. . . . Give us this day our daily bread. . . . Deliver us from evil. . . ." Then to my surprise they chanted the "Salve Regina" in Latin—*"Salve Regina, mater Misericordia Vita dulcedo . . ."*

I joined in.

Indeed, on this voyage through unknown seas,

we have to have faith—in God, and also in ourselves.

In the friary, where I grew up, I had a small room all my own. I soon learned, however, that here on board, only the Captain General had a small cabin and a bunk in which to sleep. The rest of us had no special place.

As darkness fell, all hands, excepting those on duty, lay down on deck for the night. Luis and I, and the three other gromets, curled up together like puppies close to the mast, and were soon asleep.

The breeze was gentle. The sea was calm. The *Niña*, the *Pinta*, the *Santa María* sailed quietly westward, through the night.

7 September. Day 2. I awakened before | *Surprises* dawn. At first I did not know where I was. Then, | seeing sleeping seamen around me, looking like mounds in the half dark, and feeling the swell of the sea below us, I remembered. Quietly, I pulled a blank book and a pencil from my duffle bag.

Brother Ernesto had given them to me. "Here, my son," he had said. "Write down all that you

13

see, all that you do. Who knows what marvelous things you will encounter. And it is easy, as days go by, to forget." He smiled. "I myself have never even left the island of Gomera. We will all be waiting for you. And praying for you."

Brother Ernesto. His kind gray eyes. How often I had looked into them when I was afraid. When I was sick. When I was uncertain. And he never failed me. Never having known my father, I do not know the feelings that sons and fathers have for each other. But I do not think they could be stronger than the bond between me and Brother Ernesto. Now I will not fail him. I will write down everything.

I leaned against the base of the mast, and with the book on my knees, I began to write the events of the past two days. It is a good thing I was brief. Because in ten minutes' time a clear voice lifted in song:

>   *Blessed be the light of day,*
>   *and the Holy Cross, we say.*
>   *Blessed be the immortal soul*
>   *And the Lord who keeps it whole. . . .*

The men and boys around me stirred. I stashed my writing equipment back in my bag, and looked around. Luis was gone. One of the other gromets looked at me sleepily.

"Where is Luis?" I asked.

The boy cupped his ear with his hand, then pointed toward the stern.

The song over, the voice now recited the "Hail Mary." "Hail Mary, full of grace, the Lord is with thee. . . ."

It was Luis.

I struggled up to join in the morning prayer. My back was stiff. My life at the friary was not one of great luxury. But there at least I did have a bed.

I never knew so much praying went on on shipboard. And I did not know I would have to sleep outside, on the deck. Well, growing up in a friary, I was used to praying. And I suppose after some time I will get used to sleeping on deck as well. Still, I wondered. What new surprises would I get today?

Food was being given out near the aft hatch. More biscuits, cheese, and fruit. Someone poked me. "Don't worry. We will get something better later on."

It was Luis.

"I had the night watch. From three to seven," he explained. "It is the worst. It's so hard to stay awake. I'm going to sleep now."

I wondered: Does anyone in charge know I'm here? What am I supposed to be doing? As if in answer to my unspoken thought, Luis pointed.

"See him?" He pointed to a short husky seaman with bushy eyebrows. "That is Maestro Gabriel. He is in charge of the gromets. He will explain our duties." Luis ducked away, yawning.

"You're the new boy? Come along."

Soon I was walking alongside the husky seaman.

"What do you know about ships, lad?"

I explained that I have been in fishing boats, and once in an open whaling boat. And that my father had been a seaman.

He nodded, perhaps assuming I had learned about life at sea on my father's knee. I did not have a chance to add that I never even knew my father. I hope Maestro Gabriel does not now think I know more than I do.

He led me up three steps at the stern, to the poop deck.

A large compass is mounted on a wooden stand called a binnacle. The officer of the watch stays on the poop deck. I was surprised to learn that the helmsman, who works the tiller that steers the ship, is not up here, but down below. The officer calls out the direction. The helmsman below then moves the tiller accordingly.

We climbed below. It was a gloomy place, dimly lit. I had hoped to watch the helmsman at work. But since the wind had died down, we were hardly moving. So there was no steering to be done. Maestro Gabriel and I climbed back up to the poop deck.

"Now, lad, pay attention. Watch the ampolleta."

Maestro Gabriel pointed to a sandglass. At the moment the last bit of sand fell from the top half to the bottom, a gromet who stood nearby turned the glass. The officer made a stroke on a slate to record the half hour that had passed.

One watch lasts for four hours. It is divided into eight half-hour periods. Now, as it was the fifth half hour of the watch, the gromet sang out:

Five is past, and six floweth,
More shall flow if God willeth,
Count and pass, make voyage fast.

Finishing, the gromet gave me a wink.

Maestro Gabriel motioned to me. I followed him off the poop deck.

"Can you remember all that?" he asked. For an answer I repeated the verse I had just heard. "Good!" He went on, "There is a different ditty for each half hour. Stay up on the poop deck, listen, and try to remember them."

I nodded.

"One more thing. How well do you know your prayers, lad?"

I recited the Lord's Prayer for him. Then the "Hail Mary." Then, for good measure, I sang the "Salve Regina" straight through. (I sang the whole of it, which is longer than what we sang last night on deck.)

Maestro Gabriel looked at me, astonished.

"How do you know all that?"

I told him I had grown up in the friary.

He took off his red wool hat and scratched his head. He seemed amused at something. "Well! I can see now why Captain Pinzón took you on. You looked a little spindly to me."

Spindly! Sure, I am skinny—but strong!

"We'll see, then." He left me abruptly, walking toward the forward deck.

I shook my head. He was not the only one astonished. I was not taken on this voyage because I could row and climb and work hard. I was hired because I could sing! Whatever the reason, I am not sorry. I headed back to the poop deck.

While I learned verses up on the poop deck, I got to know my fellow gromets as each, in turn, came on duty. In addition to Luis and myself, there is Pepe and Diego and Manuel. Pepe, though fat, has a high squeaky voice—which surprised me. I don't know why, but I expected a wide body to produce a deep voice.

Diego is skinny, like me. He has stiff black hair and long fingers, and is good at tying knots. (He showed me some at the end of his watch. He carries a piece of line around with him so he can work on it and practice knots.) But he sometimes forgets parts of the ditties. Maybe I can help him with the ditties (when I get to know them well myself) and he can help me with the knots.

Manuel is the tallest and oldest gromet. He sings in a lusty, enthusiastic manner. His voice is strong, but not fine. He is the one who winked at me on the poop deck. And of course there is Luis. He is short and sturdy, with black curly hair. He sings well, with feeling. He always looks on the bright side of things. And his happy outlook shows in his singing.

By day's end I thought I knew most of the verses. While there was still some light, I went midship and wrote the verses in my book, to help me remember. Then I stowed the book in my bag.

I wondered whether I would get seasick. There was no way to tell yet, because at first the sailing was smooth. And since then there has been little wind. At times the sea was as calm as a millpond. The three ships sat without moving. The sails hung motionless. I had thought the Captain General would be storming and fuming at the delay. Since he spent most of his time on the poop deck, I had a good chance to observe him. But to my surprise, he seemed calm and not un-happy—maybe because all three vessels were becalmed alike, not just the *Santa María*. No one was beating us out.

As I lay down for my second night's sleep, the deck was as steady as a bed.

Abruptly, in the middle of the night, this changed. A stiff wind from the northeast blew up. The deck tilted sharply to the port side; we rolled and tumbled against each other. It was about three in the morning. I knew the time because men were getting up for the three-to-seven watch. I slept on and off till daybreak.

8 September. Day 3. When I awoke, the big square sail above was filled. At last we had some good wind. We should sail well today and make up for yesterday. But soon there was another problem. We were taking in too much water. The bilge (the lowest part of the hold) was filling, causing the *Santa María* to wallow and roll. Also, if water gets to our stores, they will rot. There is a pump down in the bilge, but it did not work fast enough. So every man not needed for the sailing of the ship (including me) was busy bailing. Buckets were filled in the bilge, passed along, dumped, then handed down again.

The bilge

21

It stank down in the bilge. We stood knee deep in water. Dead insects, and sometimes a rat, floated by. We took turns down there. No one could stay for long. In addition to the stink, the ship's rolling is worse down below.

It was a long, wearying day. But at least I had the answer to my question: Did I get seasick? No. Only a little dizzy. Poor Diego, though, so eager to be a grown-up full seaman, had a terrible time, vomiting again and again over the rail.

Except for Diego, we all bailed till our arms ached. At nightfall, after evening prayers, I heard two of the officers talking. Even with strong winds, it seems, we logged only twenty-seven miles today. How can we reach the Indies at this rate? They fear the *Santa María* is not seaworthy enough to make the voyage of 2,400 miles.

I was too tired to write any more in my book. Too tired to even worry. One minute I was looking up at the stars; the next minute I was asleep. I awoke once. At the change of the night watch I heard Pepe's shrill voice drift through the darkness:

> *The watch is called,*
> *the glass floweth.*
> *We shall make a good voyage,*
> *if God willeth.*

Amen! I smiled and fell back asleep.

9 September. Day 4. We are sailing briskly, with a good wind from the east. Miracle of miracles, we are no longer taking in water. The sun is shining. Everyone seems cheerful. Now, at last, things will be as they should be.

"We will never see land again!"

I stood on the poop deck, observing the gromets' duties: the verse singing, the turns of the ampolleta. These may sound like trivial things, but I soon saw that they are important. Everything must be done with precision. The ampolleta-turning is the only way we have to know how much time has passed. It cannot be done a moment too late, or too soon. And the verse singing? I have the feeling it does something to cheer the men.

The gromets also help out with various tasks. The one I like best is helping Francisco, the seaman in charge of the food. We help him prepare

23

the soup, tend the fire, bring up the stores, cut up the cheese.

I am getting to know the ship's routine. And I am happy to learn that we are not going to live, day after day, on a diet of biscuits and hunks of cheese. At eleven in the morning, at the start of the second watch, we have our one hot meal.

The cooking is done on deck, on a bed of sand, in a firebox (to protect the wooden deck) with a hood above it (to protect the fire from the wind). Usually we have soup, lentil or bean, cooked in a huge copper pot. The men about to go on duty are the first to get their food.

At other times we eat cheese, salted beef, sardines or anchovies, and biscuits. While it still lasts, we also have fruit: apricots, oranges, bananas, peaches. In their spare time, the men fish. If they have any luck, we eat fish as well.

We have forty-one men on board (including the gromets). On each four-hour watch there is a lookout at the prow, one aft, and one up in the crow's nest. There is also a helmsman, and of course men to work the sails. Others clean the deck, mend sails, and make repairs of various sorts. After four in the afternoon no more cleaning chores are done. It is then that the men fish, ɔr wash their clothes in buckets.

A number of us on board are not seamen. Rodrigo de Escobedo, the Secretary of the Fleet. Luis de Torres, the Interpreter. Juan de la Cosa, the ship's owner. Diego de Arana, the Master-at-Arms. Rodrigo Sánchez, the Comptroller. Pedro Gutiérrez, Majordomo of the Spanish Royal Court, now our Chief Steward in charge of supplies.

So during the day the regular seamen must work just about every other watch. They have a name for the non-seamen. They call them "the idlers." (This name does not of course refer to the Captain General.)

This was our fourth day at sea. Everything was fine till late afternoon, when suddenly there was a big commotion on deck. Until then we could see, far behind us, the Pico de Tiede, the highest peak on the Canary Islands. Now that too has dropped beyond the horizon. We are completely out of sight of all land.

Becoming aware of this, the seamen dropped their work and ran to the rail. Some sank to the deck in prayer. Some sighed and groaned. Others wept and cried out.

"We will never see land again!"

"Good-bye, forever, my beloved Carmelita!"

We have now lost every connection with the rest of the world. We are truly alone. Heading for unknown seas. Most people know there is no truth to the old idea that the earth is flat and that it is possible to fall off. Still, the men could not help but think about it.

Hoping to calm everybody, the Captain General gathered us all together and made a comforting speech, saying what a fine crew we are, and how well rewarded we will be when we reach the rich lands of the Indies. The men calmed down after a while, and set about their duties. But except for the ever-cheerful Luis, even the gromets looked gloomy.

To me it is still a great adventure. Sitting with my back against the mainmast, I read through the verses that I had written down in my book. I am pretty sure I know them. When is Maestro Gabriel going to assign me to a watch?

Friends | **10 September. Day 5.** The day is fair. We gromets sit on deck and talk. Manuel and Diego are from Palos. They have both been to sea

26

before. When Diego talks about it, his eyes light up. "I wanted to go to sea when I was eight," he said. "But they wouldn't take me on." We all looked at each other. Even now Diego is skinny and short. How did he look three years ago?

Pepe is from Seville. His father is a cobbler. "I wanted to do something different," Pepe says, "before I settle down and sit in the shop making shoes for the rest of my life."

Luis is here to make his fortune. Then he wants to go back and farm.

"And you?" they asked me.

I told them about my life in the friary.

I want to start doing more work, I tell them. They all laugh. "Don't worry," they say. "Do you think we will let you be an idler for long?"

I never had friends my own age before. I like it.

11 September. Day 6.   Today I made friends with a seaman named Bartolomé. I helped him paint the batel—the small boat that is lashed to the deck. I learned some surprising things from him. He told me he was in prison. By volunteering for this voyage, he was given amnesty and let out of prison. He seems like a gentle man. I wondered what his crime was. He soon told me. It seems that he and three others had tried to help a friend break out of prison. They were caught and put in prison themselves. The three others are also in the crew. He points them out: Alonso, Juan, and Pedro.

I wondered why more prisoners had not volunteered. "They were afraid," said Bartolomé.

I find all this surprising. I had the idea it was a great privilege to come on this voyage. And also that the seamen were an experienced crew, the best that could be found. Now Bartolomé tells me he was a silversmith, and has never before been to sea. It was so hard to get seamen to come on this voyage, Captain Pinzón, who hired most of the crew, had to bribe prisoners to come in order to get enough men.

What else would I find out about this unusual voyage? Was I foolish for signing on?

This afternoon, Maestro Gabriel took me aside and asked if I knew the verses. This, then, was my test. He seemed surprised that I knew them all.

"How can you remember them so well?"

I told him that I wrote them down right away, so I could study them. I showed him my book. He was astonished even further to find that I could read and write. Most of the seamen could not. He looked at my book carefully. He saw that I had noted other details about the voyage, about the bilge and the distance traveled the day before: only twenty-seven miles.

At last I got a little smile from him. With a lift of his bushy eyebrows, he said, "You even have your own log, I see. . . .

"You take the seven-to-eleven watch after Pepe." He nodded and walked off. He is not a man to talk much, but I had the idea he was pleased.

I could hardly wait till seven. It would be easier for the others now, too. Before, the gromet poop-deck schedule went like this:

> *Luis* 3–7 A.M.
> *Manuel* 7–11 A.M.
> *Diego* 11 A.M.–3 P.M.
> *Pepe* 3–7 P.M.
> *Luis* 7–11 P.M.
> *Manuel* 11 P.M.–3 A.M.

29

And so on. So two gromets would have two watches in a twenty-four-hour period. My coming into the schedule would stretch it out a bit.

I got to the poop deck early. Pepe turned the ampolleta at seven, sang his final verse, then stayed on a bit as I began my first watch. I don't know whether it was due to his own good nature or whether Maestro Gabriel had asked him to stay to see if I needed any help.

As the first half hour went by, I kept my eye on the ampolleta. When the last grain of sand dropped, I turned the glass, then sang the appropriate verse. The officer of the watch made a slash mark on the board to note the half hour that had passed.

At nightfall I lit the binnacle lamp and sang the prayer verse:

> *God give us a good night and good sailing,*
> *May our ship make a good passage,*
> *Sir Captain and Master and good company . .*

Out of the corner of my eye I spied Maestro Gabriel, red cap in hand, nodding. I guess I was doing all right.

12 September. Day 7. The sea is smooth, the wind steady. We continue to sail due west. In a light breeze, we make between three and five knots. In a stronger wind, we move along at up to ten knots.

The wind changes very often. So our speed is checked every half hour. This is the way we do it.

A little wood chip a half inch thick and six inches long is thrown overboard into the water at the bow. It is attached to a thin line that has a knot in it every forty-seven feet and three inches. The wood chip is allowed to drift for twenty-eight seconds. (We count out the seconds by doing a certain chant.) As the ship sails forward, ahead of the chip, line is let out. If it is let out three rope-knots during this time, it shows we are going at a speed of three knots. If it goes out faster—say, five rope knots—it means we are sailing at a speed of five knots. I wonder who figured this system out.

Note: When we talk about ship speed, we say *knot*. When we talk about distance, we say *mile*. 1 knot = 1 nautical mile per hour.

Remember!

Cristóbal Colón, the Captain General, spends most of his time on the poop deck. As I finished singing out a verse on my second watch, he gave me a long look. Does he remember me and my canaries from San Sebastián?

The Captain General has his own way of judging speed. He watches wave foam as it hits the side of the ship, and sees how long it takes for a batch of foam to get from the bow to the stern. By this method, he can tell how fast we are going. The officers marvel at his ability. They say he is one of the great navigators of all time. He has such a keen sense of smell, they say, he can *smell* a storm coming. Both the officers and the men respect and admire him. I know I do.

We have now been at sea for a week.

13 September. Day 8. Every evening, after prayers, the Captain General announces our progress. Yesterday we logged ninety-nine miles. The day before we did even better; we averaged seven and a half knots and traveled 180 miles.

Today again the wind was good. But strong currents were pushing us sideways (this is called "crabbing"), causing us to lose headway. Still, we traveled ninety-nine miles.

According to the Captain General, our voyage is now one-third done. He has figured it should take us three weeks to cross the sea and reach Cipangu. That means only two more weeks to go.

The men cheer at the news. Luis throws his cap in the air. It nearly goes overboard.

I notice that the Captain General speaks with an accent. I asked about this.

"Sure," said Luis. "He was born in Italy. Still, his Spanish is good, for a foreigner. Don't you think?"

I agreed.

14 September. Day 9. Another good day. We sail steadily to the west. The *Niña* and *Pinta* are always in sight, sometimes quite close to us. They are able to go faster. But we stay together for two reasons. 1. If for some reason one vessel sinks, the men can board the others. 2. There is safety in numbers. Though once or twice we have sighted other ships in the distance, none has come near us. Pirates are much less likely to attack three vessels (three *armed* vessels) than one

The canary boy

that is sailing alone.

Sitting on deck in a quiet moment, enjoying the sunshine and cool breeze, Diego and I had a long talk. He told me about the ships.

The *Niña* and *Pinta* are both a class of ship called a caravel—they are smaller, faster, more streamlined than the *Santa María,* which is a cargo vessel.

The *Niña* is the swiftest, and smallest—only sixty-seven feet long. There are twenty-four men on board. Her captain is Vincente Pinzón. Originally, the *Niña* had a lateen rig (with a triangular mainsail). But in preparation for this voyage, it was changed to be square-rigged—given a large, square mainsail called a redonda. The Captain General had insisted on this change. He knew that in our journey westward we would have constant easterly winds, from behind us. When the wind comes from behind, a big square redonda gives you the most speed.

The *Pinta,* also square-rigged, is seventy feet long, with twenty-six men on board. Her captain is Martin Pinzón, the brother of Vincente Pinzón.

Both caravels were taken by the Crown from

the sea town of Palos, on the coast of Spain. The town was being punished for something. Diego did not know what.

The owners of the two caravels are also on board: Juan Nino on the *Niña*, and Cristóbal Quintero on the *Pinta*. Neither is happy about this voyage. They are afraid they will lose their ships, and maybe their lives as well.

The *Santa María* was rented for the voyage. It is big (seventy-seven feet long), but it is slow and clumsy. It was built for carrying cargo, not for speed, and we often wallow rather than cutting through the sea like the two sleek caravels. The ship's owner, Juan de la Cosa, is on board. Like the two other owners, he is not happy about this voyage. But how could he say "no" to the King and Queen?

The *Niña*, the *Pinta*, and the *Santa María* sailed from Palos on August 3. But only three days later the *Pinta*'s rudder slipped out of its socket. The Captain General was sure that Quintero, the *Pinta*'s owner, had arranged for someone to break it—so his ship would not have to go on this trip.

It seems his plan—if it *was* a plan—nearly

worked. The Captain General tried to get a ship to replace the *Pinta*. But he could not find one.

"But we fooled him!" Diego grinned. "Captain Pinzón tied the rudder together, and the *Pinta* was able to get to Grand Canary Island. There our carpenters made a new rudder. The *Niña*'s rigging was changed, and the *Pinta* was recaulked. No more leaks!

"But it took time. That's why we had to load up with more supplies when we got to *your* island. . . . You know the story from there!"

It is amazing how Diego remembers every detail about the ships. Much better than he remembers the verses and prayers!

I, in turn, told him about the Canary Islands. He was interested to hear that they are named not for the canaries there, but from the Latin word "canis," meaning dog. This is because when the islands were first discovered, there were wild dogs there. The birds got their name because they lived on the islands.

I told him about the canaries that we raise. How we have older birds, called "campaninis," who teach the young birds how to sing. How canaries can learn to imitate songs of other birds.

How they can be taught to whistle songs. Even imitate musical instruments.

As I was telling all this to Diego, I got homesick all of a sudden. So I whistled a canary song, to cheer myself up.

As I whistled away, the sun was blocked by a shadow. The Captain General was standing over us. There was, for once, a big smile on his face. "Now I remember," he said. "You are the canary boy!"

Diego and I jumped to our feet. "Don't stop. I like it." To our amazement, the Captain General sat down with us, leaning his back against the batel. "Go on. Whistle," he said. I proceeded to give him a canary-song concert. The seamen all around were listening as well.

He sat there for about ten minutes. It is the most relaxed I have ever seen him. Getting up, finally, he said, "I should have bought that canary of yours, son." Then he walked off. Diego and I stared at each other. "Do you think he noticed me?" Diego asked. "Maybe I should learn some of your canary songs!"

We whistled a bit more till we had to help Bernardino swab the deck. We whistled as we

swabbed. Bernardino joined in. We dipped our twig brooms into the pail and swabbed back and forth in rhythm. Other sailors joined in.

A good day.

I almost forgot. Sixty miles today.

15 September. Day 10. I had the worst shift today—three in the morning to seven. At daybreak I heard shouts of alarm. A meteorite had streaked across the sky. I did not see it, as I was busy turning the ampolleta. They say the meteorite blazed for a moment, then fell into the sea. *The meteorite*

"Did you see how close it was?"

"Not fifteen miles from us!"

"What if it had hit!"

"It's a bad omen!"

"Sure to mean bad luck!"

Sailors are among the most religious of men. They are also the most superstitious. The Captain General gathered the men together, telling them he has seen many such meteorites streak through the sky; that it is an act of nature, meaning neither good luck nor bad. They seemed more calm after his talk.

As he climbed back to the poop deck, I heard

him mutter to himself, "By San Fernando, I never did see one come so close!"

Navigation lesson **16 September. Day 11.** Though the wind is not strong, it is steady. So we made good progress today—117 miles. During the day the weather was not pleasant. There were storm clouds above, and drizzle now and again. Now and then, we see clumps of yellow weeds drifting by. They must be from some small island, since we are still quite far from the Indies.

I had the night watch, from eleven to three in the morning. The sky was clear. The stars sparkled above. Our pilot, Sancho Ruíz, decided to give me a lesson in navigation.

"See the North Star?" He pointed to the bright star at the end of the handle of the Little Dipper. "Stretch out your arm and point to it.

"Now point to the horizon-where the sea meets the sky."

I moved my arm.

"No, no," he said. "With one hand point to the North Star, with the other point to the horizon."

40

I stretched out both arms.

"The angle between your arms shows our latitude—how far we are above the equator. What do you judge it to be?" he asked me.

I looked at the compass. I know that with one arm straight up and one straight to the side, the angle is 90 degrees. Half of that is 45 degrees. And the angle made by my arms was about half of that.

"Twenty-three degrees north latitude?" I said.

"Not bad," he said.

Every four hours he plots our course on a chart. He unrolled it now, and made a dot to show where we were.

I looked over his shoulder. We are still closer to the Canaries than to Cipangu. Soon I had to turn my attention back to my own duty. As the last sand trickled down to the bottom of the ampolleta, I turned it, then sang out:

> *To our God let's pray*
> *to give us good voyage. . . .*
> *Protect us from the waterspout,*
> *and send no tempest nigh.*

17 September. Day 12. Another good day. The current has changed direction. It is now pushing us forward—150 miles today.

Early this morning, Luis and I were standing by the rail. We are beginning to see more and more weeds in the sea. Long stalks, with star-shaped little flowers on them.

He kept yelling, "Look!" and leaning over the rail. "It's like the river grass at home, by the Río Guadalquivir.

"Julio! Look at that!" He leaned so far over, I grabbed his shirt, just in case. Then I looked where he was pointing. There was a small crab, climbing through the weeds.

"A sure sign of land! Keep your eyes open, my friend!"

The sailors have been talking about an island they call Antilia. It is said to be in this part of the ocean. Everyone is cheerful. We all keep a sharp lookout.

Many porpoises leap up and down in the water, escorting our ship. The men managed to harpoon one. I know it provides food. Still, I am sorry. They have such a joyous look about them.

Later, after prayers, I saw the Captain General

standing alone, with head bent. I heard him whisper: "Almighty God, in whose hands are all victories, deliver us soon to land."

Today, day and night, we logged 141 miles.

18 September. Day 13.   The *Pinta* has darted ahead of us. This puts the Captain General in a foul mood. He stomps about on the deck. Martin Pinzón may be the captain of the *Pinta*. But he, Cristóbal Colón, is still Commander of the Fleet!

The sea is smooth as a river. We see great flights of birds moving west. At sundown, Pinzón had the *Pinta* lay to, facing into the wind, and waited for us to catch up. Soon we are close enough to shout back and forth.

Pinzón sounds excited. He thinks he sees land to the north. The officers and crew want to change our course from west to north. But the Captain General said, "I am not going to waste time. There is no land in that direction." Instead, he ordered that the small topsails be taken down, because the wind was now so strong. Manuel and I folded and stowed the sails. While bending down, doing this, we overheard a conversation between Juan de la Cosa and Diego de Arana, our Master-at-Arms.

"Again he is annoyed with Pinzón."

"It is because Pinzón is independent and has his own ideas."

"*He* doesn't like that."

"Pinzón is smart . . ."

"Does he want a dummy to command the *Pinta*? You know that without the Pinzóns, he could not even have gotten a crew. Now he acts like a king!"

They moved away, and we didn't hear any more.

Manuel and I looked at each other. They were talking about the Captain General. He is in charge. Don't they understand that?

19 September. Day 14. Today there was no wind. For hours we were almost becalmed. We made a sounding, to see how deep the sea is here. We let out the line for twenty fathoms, but could not find bottom.

At nightfall, the three ships drew together. The Captain General wanted to know the position calculated by each pilot. Our pilot, Sancho Ruíz, calculated we are now 1,200 miles west of the Canaries. Cristóbal Salmiento, pilot on the *Pinta*, has calculated a bit more: 1,260 miles. Peralonso on the *Niña* reckons we have sailed 1,320 miles.

I caught a glimpse of our chart, showing our present position. No matter who is right, we are still nowhere near land.

Thick weeds | **20 September. Day 15.** This morning as the sun rose, three tiny birds flew right over us, singing as they went. The sight of them made everyone cheerful. Yet today something else began to happen. The clumps of weeds got thicker and thicker. They spread around us, looking like a green meadow. There was little wind. Soon we could barely push through them. Everyone began to worry. Would we get stuck in them? At night, when we went to sleep, we were not moving at all.

21 September. Day 16. There are some breaks in this meadow-on-the-sea. There, the water is clear blue. In late afternoon, as I finished my watch, I saw something like a fountain, shooting up from the sea. It was a whale, blowing water through its blowhole. The men saw it and let out a shout. The sight of it seemed to cheer them up. They then went about their tasks more briskly.

22 September. Day 17.   Third day in the weeds. Pepe and I were on food duty. We carried up cheese and biscuits from the hold. Francisco had given us special orders. No anchovies today. And no dried beef. Is he worried that our food will not last?

The men looked glum as they took their food rations. That question was on everybody's mind.

23 September. Day 18.   At last! The wind picked up. We have pushed our way through the weeds into clear seas. Sixty-six miles today. Not so much. But we are happy just to be moving.

25 September. Day 20.   This is it! I knew it would happen. At sunset, the lookout on the *Pinta* shouted, "Land ho!"   *"Land ho!"*

The Captain General fell to his knees to thank God. He asked that we sing "Gloria in Excelsis

47

Deo." The men bellowed out the prayer with great enthusiasm. They held their red caps in their hands.

Afterward, some of the men climbed up the rigging to try and get a look. Diego got up on Manuel's shoulders. Pepe and I ran to the prow. But the sun soon dropped. The sky got dark. We will have to wait until morning to see anything.

26 September. Day 21. At daybreak we scanned the horizon. But in the clear morning light, there was nothing. It was a false alarm. What they thought was land was nothing but a dark storm cloud.

Sancho Ruíz told us that storm clouds often look just like land.

The air is sweet and balmy, the sea is smooth; we cut through the water with no effort. But no one is happy. We have been at sea three weeks. The Captain General had said we would reach Cipangu in three weeks.

Flying fish with little wings leap over the sea. They sometimes land on deck. But they are no good to eat. Later on, some big dorado fish swim near the ships. The men harpoon a few. The thought of fresh fish stew tomorrow morning cheers them a little . . . but not much.

3 October 1492. Day 28.   Where are we? How far have we gone? The *Niña*'s pilot judges we have sailed 1,620 miles. Sancho Ruíz has figured 1,851. The pilot of the *Pinta* has figured 1,902 miles. The Captain General nodded at each. Then he said, "I think we've done even better than that." But he did not give an exact number. *Where are we?*

On the poop deck later on, the Captain General was sitting and writing. I was standing by the ampolleta. In his own log, I saw him write the number 2,379.

I was startled. Is that how far he thinks we have gone? I wonder why he did not say so before. If he is right, we are practically there!

6 October. Day 31.   For three days now, the wind has been very strong. We have sailed almost five hundred miles more. Why have we not reached Cipangu? Did we miss it? Is that possible? Or is it much farther away than anyone thinks? If that is true, will our food and water hold out? *An odd discovery*

49

We have now been at sea for a month. The Captain General told us the voyage would be three weeks. The men are very upset. Many times, Diego de Arana, the Master-at-Arms, has to break up fights between them. They are hungry. And they are scared. They feel trapped.

Last night I discovered something else that makes me very uneasy. I was helping Salcedo, the Captain General's servant. While I was in the Captain General's cabin, his log fell from a table. Picking it up, I saw the day's entry:

> Course due west.
> Made 171 miles between day and night.

Yet at evening prayers the Captain General announced to us that we had gone 135 miles.
He lied to us. Why?
Maybe he just made a mistake. . . .

Julio's secret | **7 October. Day 32.** Feeling disloyal, today I peeked again at the Captain General's personal log. It said: "9 knots for 2 hours. 6 knots for 8½ hours. 69 miles until an hour before sunset."

Yet at evening prayers, he announced to the

crew that we have sailed fifty-four.

My heart is troubled. Why is he lying?

Brother Gustavo once told me: Write things down if you have a problem. Seeing them there helps to understand them. Better than having them buzzing around in your head.

So I write:

Question 1. How far have we really sailed?

Question 2. *Why* is the Captain General telling us wrong numbers? He is making it seem that we have sailed less far than we have. Why?

Question 3. Has he been doing this for the whole voyage?

I don't know the answer to any of these. I do know this: If the answer to three is "yes," it means my own diary is all wrong. Because I have been taking my numbers from what he announces each night.

I say nothing about this to anybody. In fact, I am not talking very much now. I am afraid I will let something slip.

"You look like you have a secret," Luis remarked.

It makes me feel bad. I am keeping an important secret from my friends. But what can I do? I do not want to be disloyal to the Captain General. I am caught in the middle. I don't like it.

Tonight the Captain General gave us special orders. Every man is to be on deck at sunrise. The air is very clear then. It will be easier to sight land. He tells us that the first man to sight land will get a reward of ten thousand maravedies.

Extra lookouts are posted through the night. We must be close.

I had the eleven-to-three watch. The Captain General spent the entire watch on the poop deck. He sat on a small stool and wrote in his log. Then he looked up at me.

"They tell me, son, you know how to read and write."

"Yes, sir. The Franciscan Brothers taught me."

"I left my son Diego with the Franciscan Brothers near Palos."

"He will be happy there," I said.

"How old are you, son?"

"Twelve."

"And what is your name?"

"Julio de la Vega Medina, sir."

"I could not read or write when I was your age," the Captain General told me. "I taught myself, when I was older. . . . I taught myself to read Latin, too. Because all the great scholars and geographers write in Latin."

He closed his log and looked up at the night sky. I thought our conversation was over, when he suddenly said, "A man can do so much more when he can read. . . ."

"Yes, sir."

"You have the chance to learn about the thoughts and ideas of all the great men of the world—not just those close to you. Here. Look at this." He picked up a book from the deck. "See this?"

I read aloud: *"Imago Mundi* by Pierre d'Ailly."

The Captain General nodded. "He says here, 'The ocean is not very wide, and can be navigated in a few days with a fair wind.' "

In the dim light I could see he had made notes all along the margins of the book.

"And that great thinker Aristotle said this: 'Between the end of Spain and the beginning of the Indies is a small sea, navigable in a few days. . . .' "

He got up and paced around the poop deck. "Why, even the Bible says: 'Six parts hast thou dried up.' Do you know what that means, son?"

I opened my mouth to answer, but the Captain General went on. "It means the ocean covers only one seventh of the globe. So it *cannot* be very wide! You see how knowing all this has given me faith to make this voyage? Still . . ." He frowned. I looked at him. Did he have doubts himself? Then his mood seemed to change. He leaned on the rail. "How fast do you think we are going, son?"

"I don't know, sir."

He put his arm around my shoulder. "See that wave, breaking at the bow?"

I nodded.

"Watch it."

Several moments went by.

"Now. You see, the wave has reached the stern. I judge," he said, "we are sailing at seven knots."

"How do you know that, sir?"

"Experience." He smiled at me. "That is one thing I did not learn from reading books!"

I could hardly believe that we were having this talk. With the faith he has, and his knowledge, how could I have doubted him? How can anyone doubt him? He is truly great. I know it.

I had to get back to my own duties. All the while, I had to keep glancing at the ampolleta. When the last grain went down, I turned it.

The officer of the watch made a mark on the board. I sang out the verse into the night. At three, when I left, the Captain General was still sitting there in the dark.

Not many men were sleeping. Each hoped to be the first to sight land. They prowled on the deck and stared over the ocean.

Diego was standing at the bow.

"Do you think if a gromet sees land first, he will get the reward?" he asked.

I answered, "Why not?"

I have written these notes by moonlight. I did not want to forget one word of my talk with the Captain General. Now I, for one, am going to sleep. Good night.

8 October. Day 33. At sunrise, the Captain General reminded us of the reward money. As he was speaking, the *Niña*, a bit ahead of us, fired a cannon and ran a flag up the mast. This was the sign. It meant they had sighted land! *Follow the birds*

We sailed ahead hopefully. But by evening we knew the truth. It was another false alarm.

The Captain General does not even seem discouraged. Instead, he stares up at the darkening sky. Large flocks of birds are flying toward the southwest. Ducks, gulls, terns. And land birds as well as seabirds. For the first time he orders that we change course. No longer do we go due west. Following the birds, we now sail southwest.

All night long, we hear them overhead. How many there are! Surely they will lead us to land.

9 October. Day 34. The men care nothing for birds. They stand in groups, grumbling. They are sure we are lost. They are calling the Captain General a madman. *"Throw him overboard!"*

"We are running out of water. . . ."

"And food. . . ."

"We will have to throw the crazy foreigner overboard. . . ."

"I will do it myself . . . this very night . . ."

"Then at least we can try to get back home. To go on is crazy!"

Would they dare? It makes no sense. Surely we are closer to the Indies now than to the Canary Islands. Turning back now, we will be certain to starve to death.

10 October. Day 35.   I did not sleep well last night. I kept listening for a splash in the darkness. But in the morning, the Captain General was on the poop deck as usual.

"Tierra!" **11 October. Day 36.**   The biscuits are rotten. Our water is stale. The men get even more surly. They work so slowly, they do practically nothing. Pepe and I thought we saw a branch with green leaves on it. But it disappeared so fast, we weren't sure.

At day's end, after prayers, the Captain General made a special thanksgiving: "We thank God for giving us new hope through the many signs of land He has provided."

"What signs?"

A fat, redheaded seaman named Antonio blew his nose loudly as the Captain General spoke. Are they ready to mutiny? To take over the ship? I went to sleep very uneasy.

Before midnight, I was awakened by a poke in the back. It was Luis.

"I just got off watch," he said. "The Captain General saw a light," he whispered. "Like a torch!"

I sat up, trying not to disturb those around me.

"Did *you* see anything?"

"No."

"Did the man in the crow's nest see it?"

"No." Luis shook his head. "But still. You know the Captain General has very good eyesight."

It was hard to fall asleep again. I stared up at the stars, and at the birds overhead flying by in the moonlight.

Then it happened. Two hours later, the *Pinta*, ahead of us, fired a cannon. This meant they had sighted land. They shortened sail to let us catch up. The man in their crow's nest was shouting, "Tierra! Tierra!"

His name, we soon learned, is Rodrigo de

Triana. When we got closer, we could hear the crew of the *Pinta* chanting, "Ten thousand maravedies, ten thousand maravedies . . ."

They are happy for their crewmate.

We all agree, he is a lucky man.

All three ships haul in their sails and lay to facing into the wind.

Have we really reached the Indies?

Or is it another false alarm?

We have to wait until dawn to find out.

Part II

We Explore the Islands

12 October 1492. Day 37. It was true! *San Salvador*

Praise be to God.

It was land! No mistake this time!

First, we could not believe our eyes. Then, what a hullabaloo there was. Hats thrown in the air. Singing. Praying. Shouting.

Diego grabbed me and began hopping up and down.

"What are you doing?" I asked him.

"The morisca!" he told me. "Have you never danced the morisca?"

I told him there is not much dancing in a friary.

The land lay about six miles ahead. And a good thing we did not come closer last night. A reef lay between us and the shore. We would have run aground.

We raised our sails and sailed smartly to the south. We soon found a bay we could enter. We saw a long white beach. There seemed to be some people, almost hidden by the trees. We were not close enough to make them out clearly.

We dropped anchor and lowered the batel. The Captain General got into it. Also Señor Rodrigo de Escobedo, who is to draw up official deeds for any new lands we discover. Also Señor Rodrigo Sánchez, Comptroller from the Royal Court. He is to see to it that the King and Queen get their fair share of whatever the Captain General discovers. As though the Captain General would cheat the Crown!

The last one to get in the boat was Luis de Torres, the Interpreter. He knows Arabic and Hebrew, languages often used by traders in Eastern lands. He will, it is hoped, be able to translate what the people here have to say, and help the Captain General converse with them. De Torres is a tubby, fussy, character. The batel nearly tips over as he clumsily gets into it.

When he is finally settled, the Captain General looks up. At me! "You! Canary boy!" he calls out. "Bring down the sack of gifts."

I grab the sack and climb down into the boat.

"You can row us to shore, son."

I picked up the oars and rowed swiftly and smoothly.

Rowing, I faced the stern. As we hit the beach,

I jumped out and had my first close look at the people.

What a shock! They stood there, naked as the day they were born! They are handsome people with big eyes and dark skin. Their hair is straight and coarse, almost like a horse's mane. No one is fat-bellied. Nobody is skinny, or crooked-bodied. Some have their whole bodies painted. Some just have a dab of paint on the tip of the nose.

They seemed even more surprised at our appearance than we were at theirs. Had they never seen clothing? Or a sailing vessel?

Captain Martin Pinzón and Captain Vincente Pinzón joined us from the *Pinta* and the *Niña*. They unfurled the royal banner with its large green cross.

We all kneeled on the beach as the Captain General gave thanks to God for our safe passage. Rising, he then said: "Bear witness, all who are here today: I take possession of this island for King Ferdinand and Queen Isabella. I name it San Salvador, in the name of our Lord."

Then everyone got busy. The Secretary, Rodrigo de Escobedo, wrote official documents claiming the land.

I was instructed to give gifts to the people. I opened the sack and handed out beads and little hawk bells. The people were delighted, hanging the beads around their necks and tinkling the bells.

Luis de Torres, meanwhile, was trying to hold a conversation with the man who seems to be Chief. First he tried Arabic. No answer. Then he tried Hebrew. This does not work either. The Chief shook his head, then answered in some very different language.

I watched them. How funny the two of them looked: De Torres, in his shiny silk plum-colored clothes, standing in the sand under the palm trees, and the tall Chief, naked, with white paint dabbed on the tip of his nose. Both talking, and neither understanding the other.

I could not help laughing. Someone touched my shoulder. I turned. A boy was standing next to me. He pointed to himself and said, "Tonoro."

That must be his name.

I pointed to myself and said, "Julio."

He nodded. Then he again said, "Tonoro," and pointed to the sky, and made flapping motions.

His name, Tonoro, must mean "bird."

That made sense. Many people at home are named for animals. Leon, which means "lion." And I know a man named Perro, which means "dog." But Julio. It means "July." How could I explain "July" to him?

He bent down and patted the sand. "Guanahani," he said. Maybe it means "sand"?

I picked up some sand. "Guanahani?"

He shook his head, then motioned with both hands, over everything.

The island. It is called Guanahani. That's what he meant.

It was like a puzzle. There are so many things we do not understand about each other's lives. But there must be lots of ways we are alike.

Tonoro is taller than I am. I wonder how old he is. I started to count to twelve (my age) on my fingers. He was smiling and watching. It would take a lot of time to get to understand each other. I wish that could be. Because I know we could get to be friends.

But I did not have time. The Captain General and some of the others were about to explore the island. It was my job to row Luis de Torres back to the *Santa María*. Tonoro helped me pull the batel into the water. Then we clasped hands, and parted.

Back on the *Santa María*, Luis, Diego, Pepe, and Manuel crowded around me. I told them everything. At evening prayers, the Captain General, now returned, announced that he had named this place San Salvador in honor of our Lord. He said the island is now a possession of the Crown. And since it is off the coast of the Indies, we should call the people who live here "Indians."

The sun is setting. I lean against the mast, open my book, and describe everything that happened today while it is fresh in my mind. I am smiling as I write. We did it! We found the Indies by sailing west.

But now a question has begun to creep into my mind. If this is the land of gold and jewels, why do the people not even wear any clothes?

One last thing to note, Cristóbal Colón, the Captain General, has a new title. Now that he has discovered new lands for the Crown, he is to be called the Admiral of the Ocean Sea.

13 October. At daybreak, many Indians come to visit us on shipboard. They come in boats carved out of trees. Some are large, and carry fifty men. Some are small, with only one man. We stood at the rail and watched them approach. They do not use oars and oarlocks as we do. Instead, they dip long, flat pieces of wood into the water, and push themselves along that way. They call this kind of boat a *canoa*.

More and more arrived. They swarmed up onto the ship. Soon there were so many, some had to wait their turn below, bobbing up and down in their *canoa*s.

They brought us parrots as gifts, brilliantly colored birds of blue and purple and red and yellow. We are instructed that these people are to be treated with every courtesy. And that we are not to receive anything from them without giving a gift in return.

Some of them wear bits of gold hanging from their noses. By using sign language, the Admiral tried to find out where they got the gold. (By now he has given up on getting any help from our learned Interpreter, Señor de Torres, who has stubbornly kept on asking these people questions in Hebrew or Arabic, when it is clear they do not understand anything he says!)

Using sign language, the Indians explained that there are many islands to the southwest. And that is where the gold is from. There, they say, the people wear thick bracelets of gold on their arms and legs and necks.

They tell also of a very large island where many ships sail in and out. They call this place Colba.

The Admiral studies his charts and globes. He is soon convinced that Colba is the Indian name for Cipangu.

All day long I walked about, searching for Tonoro. I wonder why he did not come aboard with the rest. Maybe he did, and I did not see him in the crowd. I am disappointed.

In the afternoon, our Indian visitors began to leave, getting into their *canoa*s to return to their island. All except six, whom we keep on board with us, to guide us through these unknown waters on the next part of our journey.

The Admiral announced his plan to us at evening prayers. At first light, we are to set sail for Cipangu. Or, as the Indians call it, Colba.

16 October.   Today we stopped at a small island that the Admiral wished to claim for the Crown. Our Indians said (using sign language) that there was much gold here. The Admiral went ashore, and named the island Santa María de la Concepción. But he was back on board in two hours. There was no sign of gold at all.

Last night one of our Indian guides escaped by jumping overboard. While we were anchored here, a second one escaped. He jumped over the rail into the water, and was picked up by a man in a *canoa*. Diego and I saw it happen. The man in the *canoa* must have followed us all the way from San Salvador. Why would our guide want to escape?

"The Admiral plans to take them back to Spain," Diego told me.

I didn't know that.

The Indians glided off very fast. Some of our crew chased them in the batel, but could not catch them.

The Admiral is angry about it. He orders us to watch our captives very carefully from now on.

17 October.   Last night, at sunset, we sighted another island to the starboard. It was long and thin in shape. Seeing it, our four remaining Indians got excited. They began to make digging motions. This led the Admiral to believe there was a gold mine on the island.

We lay to till morning. (There were many large rocks offshore. We could not risk hitting one in the dark.) At first light we sailed closer, and the Admiral went ashore in the batel. As usual, he was accompanied by the two court officials, Escobedo and Sánchez, as well as several crewmen.

Soon the batel came back with casks of fresh water. As we hauled them up, one of the men, a thin bald man named Alvar, was giving a message to Diego de Arana, our Master-at-Arms, who listened carefully, then nodded and turned to the rest of us. "The Admiral has given us permission to go ashore for the day."

We let out a cheer and lined up at the rail. We gromets were the last to get ashore. But we didn't care. We had a whole wonderful day to explore. . . .

First we threw off our clothes and drifted in the warm blue water. Then we lay on the beach in the sun. The rest of us felt lazy. But Manuel was eager to explore. So we dressed and walked in among the trees.

I have never seen so many different kinds of trees. They have big flat leaves, and strange fruit hanging from the branches.

"Everything smells so good," said Pepe.

"Let's not get lost," said Diego.

We soon came to a clearing, and three big mastifflike dogs dashed toward us, barking.

"Don't run, or look scared," said Luis. It turned out the dogs were welcoming us, not attacking. For soon they were licking our hands.

We had come to a village. There were about ten houses, neatly constructed, with tall pointy roofs. Some people appeared and beckoned to us. Most were wearing short tunics of cotton. A few wore nothing at all. Like the Indians of San Salvador, they are handsome people, sturdy, and friendly. They began to talk to us. Of course we did not understand them. Nor they us.

"Good day," said Pepe. "How are you?"

They nodded, and waved us into a house. Inside, it was neat and fresh. There were woven nets slung from one wall to another.

We wondered what they were for. We soon got our answer. A young boy, about five, leaped into one and lay back.

"Hamaca," he said.

They sleep in them!

Soon we were all lying in these *hamaca*s.

Pepe seemed about to fall asleep in the thing, until the people began handing out some fruit. That got him up. The fruit was sweet and juicy. It was like no fruit we had ever tasted.

Manuel pulled some little hawk bells out of his pocket and handed them around. The people began tinkling away. Then one of the men gave Manuel a small spear with a fishbone for a tip. The men seemed to want to take us someplace. Maybe to go fishing. We were not sure. But we decided it was time to return to the beach. We said good-bye to these kind people, and were soon back on the *Santa María*.

The Admiral named this island Fernandina, to honor King Ferdinand.

No gold was found on Fernandina.

19 October.   Sailing through these waters, we see many bright-colored dorado fish, bright blue, yellow, red, and some even many-colored. They weigh up to one hundred pounds. On the islands themselves there seem to be no large animals, though there are lizards and many birds. On one island Martin Pinzón killed a serpent.

Sometimes we see flocks of parrots so large that the sky becomes darkened with them. But there is one thing we do not find anywhere. Gold.

23 October. The Admiral has begun to suspect that the Indians tell us there is gold on these islands so we will stop and they will have a chance to escape. He has decided we will waste no more time, but head straight for Colba, which he is now sure is Cipangu.

28 October. At sunrise we approached the northern coast of Colba. We entered the mouth of a river, where the water is deep and calm. Here we cast anchor.

Will we find what we are looking for?

Diego shinnied up the mast to see better.

He shouted down to us, "The island is so large, I cannot see the ends of it!"

We are all eager to explore.

The Garden of Eden | **29 October.** If I did not know better, I would say this is the Garden of Eden, it is so beautiful. The trees are tall, with bright flowers and fruit.

There are birds of all sizes and colors. Their songs fill the air.

There is a house close to the river. Inside, Pepe and I see fishhooks made of horn, some bone harpoons, and a net made of palm threads. These people must be fishermen. But where are they?

We saw a small dog near the house, and were surprised it did not bark at us.

Now, back on the *Santa María*, I see the shadows of the mountains all around us. I hear the crickets, which sing through the night.

31 October. We are moving on, sailing along the coast. The Admiral names every place we see. Río de la Luna [Moon River]. Cabo de Palmas [Cape of Palm Trees]. Río de Mares [River of Mars]. And to the entire island of Colba he gives the name Juana, in honor of the Prince of Castile. *Juana*

Every evening he reminds us how rich are these lands of the East. Gold, silver, precious gems, spices, and perfumes. He tells us how the great explorer Marco Polo described all these things many years ago. And remember, he says, it took *him* three years to get here. By boat to Constantinople. Then on horseback, across all of Asia.

77

And we have gotten here in little more than a month! We must just find the source of the wealth. . . .

At each place, small parties go out to explore. Near Río de Mares, we found a village. The people must have run away very suddenly, for there was even food in a bowl.

Inside some houses we saw carved statues of wood, and masks on the walls. There were some dogs running about. None of these dogs barked. We finally figured out that they cannot bark! Whoever heard of a dog like that!

As we were leaving, a man wandered in. He was startled to see us. But he did not run off. He shared some food with us. It was pale orange in color, and kind of sweet, tasting like chestnuts. He called it *ajes*. We soon took leave, and are now back on the ship.

Ajes. I must remember this new word.

Strange and interesting as everything is, can this really be Cipangu? If so, where are the roofs of gold? Where are the lords and ladies wearing silken garments woven with rubies and pearls? Where are all these things that Marco Polo saw in Cathay?

1 November. Sailing east along the coast, we hope to see Chinese junks or other signs of the Orient. We never do. But we did learn something. The people here call this land Cuba, not Colba, as the Guanahani Indians do.

Cuba

2 November. Today we got some interesting news. Three native men on the beach told us that there is much gold inland at a place called Cubanacan, where the king lives.

In search of the Great Khan

The Admiral is convinced that what they are saying is "Great Khan." (The Great Khan is the ruler of all Cathay. Great Khan means "King of Kings.") This gives him a new idea. I hear him telling Gutiérrez. Perhaps we are not in Cipangu. Perhaps we are already in Mangi, which is a southern part of Cathay! The Admiral has decided to send Luis de Torres, a seaman named Rodrigo Xeres, and a Guanahani Indian to find the Royal Court. They carry with them a Latin passport and a letter to the Great Khan.

The three Indians drew a map in the sand to show them exactly where this place is. We watched as de Torres and the others marched off into the forest. De Torres looked nervous. For

the Admiral has told us that the Great Khan keeps leopards and lions and lynxes at the Court to chase wild boar. He also has eagles that are trained to catch wolves. Poor de Torres! He is not enjoying his adventures.

4 November. As we wait for them to return, we work. We have beached the *Niña* and are busy cleaning her hull. We have spent all day scrubbing away barnacles, seaweed, and all kinds of muck. We beach only one ship at a time. The other two remain ready to sail. For safety.

6 November. De Torres and the others have returned. We gather round to listen. *Dog-faced man-eaters*

Arriving at the spot the Indians showed on their sand map, they found no Great Khan, no Imperial Palace. Instead they found only a village with fifty huts. They came back tired and muddy. "At least," Luis whispered, "there were no lions, or wolf-killing eagles!"

Is the Admiral discouraged? Of course not. He has now heard about a new place—a large island to the east, that the natives call Bohío. The remaining Indians we have on board are frightened of going to Bohio. They have heard of this place. They say there are people there called Canibales who have only one eye, and the face of a dog. And worse yet, they eat people.

We are again told to watch our Indians carefully. It is now even more likely they will try to escape. I am sorry for them. Why should they be taken from their homes and families for so long, and taken to such frightening places?

More Indian captives

11 November. Five young Indians (a bit older than I) came aboard today. The sixth remained in their *canoa*. The Admiral has ordered that we keep them with us. The sixth, seeing his friends held, sped away in the *canoa*. Later, our men brought back more Indians, this time seven women and three children. It is true. The Admiral plans to take them all back to Spain. And he feels the men would be more contented if they have some women with them. In the evening, the husband of one of the women swam out and asked to stay. Our ship is getting very crowded with Indians!

21 November. Today Captain Martin Pinzón *Babeque* has sailed away on the *Pinta* to an island called Babeque. An Indian told him that the people there gather much gold and hammer it into gold bars. He has gone without permission from the Admiral. He did not even tell him he was going. I have never seen the Admiral so angry.

We watched till the *Pinta* was a dark speck on the sea, then disappeared altogether.

5 December. We have spent more than a *A hog-faced* month now exploring Cuba. We have sailed *fish* along its coast almost four hundred miles. We have dived for oysters—but found no pearls. We caught a strange fish with a face like a hog, and a hard shell over its body. The Admiral orders us to salt it so he can take it back to show to the Queen. Diego asks: Do you think the Queen really wants to see a hard-shelled hog-faced fish?

We have walked through bamboo groves and seen palm trees and tall straight pines. We have explored many rivers. And everywhere we go, we have planted a large cross.

Last night two of our young Indians escaped. I am glad for them. (I hope the Admiral never sees this book!)

Today the *Niña* and the *Santa María* head for Bohío.

How will the *Pinta* find us?

Bohío (La Isla Española) **6 December.** At sunset we entered a harbor. The next morning we began to explore. The valleys, rivers, fields, and even the trees, such as oaks and myrtles, look like those in Spain. For that reason the Admiral has named this place La Isla Española [The Spanish Island].

10 December. We have passed some easy days, sailing along the coast. The waters are rich with all kinds of fish—salmon, pompano, eels, sardines, and shrimp—which we catch, and eat. Everyone's mood is good. From time to time we see some Indians. But they run away when they see us.

12 December. Today we set up a cross near the shore. Then three sailors headed up the mountainside to examine the trees and plants here. They soon heard voices and met with a crowd of Indians, who ran away. Our men caught one young woman and brought her back to the ship. She was surprised to see the other Indian women aboard—the ones from Cuba. She conversed with them through the night.

13 December. In the morning, we took the woman back to shore, after giving her our usual gifts—beads, brass rings, and hawk bells.

At first, she was not happy at leaving the other women. Then, seeing we meant no harm, she agreed to lead us to her village. It was very large. About one thousand houses. First the people trembled when they saw us. But soon they lost their fear, and even brought us fish and bread, which they call caçabi. The bread is made from the root vegetable they call *ajes*. Luis pulled one up (after asking permission), and said, "I wonder if we could grow these at home." He wrapped it in a palm leaf and carried it back to the ship.

Funny. These people are not dog faced, as our Indians feared they would be. And they are not fierce at all!

14 December. This morning we set sail for a small island about three miles off the coast. The | *Tortuga* people there were also afraid. On seeing our ships approach, they lit signal fires in tall towers, then fled. The Admiral has named the island Isla de la Tortuga [Tortoise Island].

There are many fields planted with *ajes*. We did not stay long. It was but a short sail back to Española.

Valley of Paradise **15 December.** There is a river that flows through a valley. It has caught the Admiral's fancy, and he wishes to explore it.

Entering the river, we find the current is so strong, we can make no headway. So our men go ashore and pull us upriver by means of a line.

Coming to a village, we see no one. Again, signal fires have been lit. The people here must have bad enemies who invade. Perhaps the dog-faced Canibales we heard of. Why else would they have watch towers, and be so fearful?

The Admiral names the place Valle del Paraíso [Valley of Paradise].

The young cacique **16 December.** At last, we met some people who are not afraid of us. It happened this way. We were sailing along in a stiff wind, when we

spied an Indian in a *canoa*. We took him aboard.
Then the Admiral asked Luis to get a bag of gifts
and give him some.

Luis handed the man some hawk bells, beads,
and about ten brass rings, and said, "Merry
Christmas!"—which made the Admiral smile.

He is right. It is almost Christmas.

We let the man off close to shore. He must
have gone straight to his people and told them
about us, because they began appearing on the
shore. Soon there were more than five hundred
of them, gazing with wonder at our ships.

Their King, who is only about twenty-one
years old, came aboard. The Admiral tries to
explain to him that we come from a great king-
dom across the sea. But the young King keeps
shaking his head and pointing to the sky. These
people have never seen sails before. They believe
our sails are wings, and we have flown down from
Heaven.

The young King and the others were as
naked as the day they were born. They are handsome people, and not shy in their nakedness.
Strange . . . we are getting used to seeing people
with no clothes on. Imagine if someone were to

walk down the streets of San Sebastián wearing no clothes!

Gold | **17 December.** The Admiral has two things in mind. One is to claim these beautiful and fertile lands for Spain. It is his thought that these people who are so gentle can be taught to work for Spain, and to wear clothing and to observe our customs. But even more important is his great desire to find gold. After evening prayers he made this announcement: "I believe," he said, "that we are very near the source of gold, and that our Lord is about to reveal its location."

What gives him this idea?

I soon found out. Manuel helped to serve the food when the young King was with the Admiral in his cabin. ("Cacique" is the name these people call their King. It is pronounced cuh-*SEEK*.)

Manuel told me the young Cacique showed the Admiral a piece of gold as big as his hand. He told the Admiral the gold came from the island of Babeque. That is where Martin Pinzón has gone in the *Pinta*. No wonder the Admiral has been looking so angry. By now, he reckons, the treacherous Pinzón has already claimed the gold.

Babeque is said to be about one hundred miles from here. We can make that in one day, with good wind.

18 December.   No wind today. So we remain at anchor. Some men have been sent out in the batel to fish with nets, while we wait.

22 December.   Wind shifts have kept us from leaving the gulf between Tortuga and La Isla Española. It was not until today, at dawn, that we finally set sail to search for the island of Babeque.

The Cacique Guacanagari

But luck was not with us. The winds became contrary, forcing us to turn back. Once again we anchored off the coast of Española. The Admiral names this new place Puerto de la Mar Santo Tomás [Port of the Sea of St. Thomas] because today is the feast day of St. Tomás.

I was standing at the rail when some Indians in a *canoa* glided up close to the ship and handed something up to me. It was a belt, with a mask hanging from it, with big ears, a tongue, and a nose—all made from hammered gold! You can be sure I took it right in to the Admiral. Meanwhile, the Indians clambered aboard and followed after me.

Using signs, the Indians told the Admiral that the splendid mask was a gift from their Cacique. Just as we have kings in different countries, the Indians have caciques in different areas. We gather that this Cacique is a great leader, who is respected far and wide. His name is Guacanagari.

Tonight, at vespers, the Admiral announced his new plan. We are not going to search for Babeque. Instead, tomorrow, we are to sail along the coast to visit the great and generous Cacique Guacanagari.

23 December.   Again no wind. We must postpone our visit to the great Guacanagari. Instead, the Admiral sent six men on foot to another village: the secretary Escobedo, four seamen, and me!

The village was about nine miles distant. It was built around a large plaza. There, thousands of people were gathered. Their Cacique received us, and gave us gifts: balls of spun cotton, small pieces of gold, and three fat geese.

When it was time to return to the ship, Indians

fought for the honor of carrying us on their shoulders. We accepted this favor only while crossing rivers and going through swamps. It was my job to carry one of the geese. Picture me—sitting on an Indian's shoulders, carrying a fat, live goose.

More than a thousand Indians came to the ships in *canoa*s, carrying gifts of fish and caçabi bread, and fresh water in earthenware jars. About five hundred more swam out, even though we are anchored three miles from shore!

Of course 1,500 Indians were not on board all at once. They came and went, taking turns. The Admiral ordered that every single one was to receive a gift. We ate fish and ajes and goose. We drank wine. Among our guests were five princes (sons of Caciques), as well as their advisors, their wives, and their children. All in all, a fine party . . . which went on quite late. . . .

24 December.   During the night, a breeze blew | *Christmas* up. Early, before sunrise, we hoisted our anchors | *Eve* and set sail. We navigated carefully, skirting a small flat island, because to the west of it lay a large reef, which could split open our hull if we hit it. Even past this, we proceeded cautiously, for on arriving here, we had noticed three sand-banks nearby. Hitting these could also do great damage. But the Admiral is a skilled navigator. Under his guidance, we were soon free and clear, heading east along the shore, toward the village of the Cacique Guacanagari.

Tomorrow is Christmas Day. I thought I would be home by now. How much longer are we going to explore? Will we ever find gold? Or the court of the Great Khan?

Christmas Day | **25 December.**   Some days in your life you never forget. For me, this was one of them.

As we sailed along the coast, the breeze was light. And by eleven at night it stopped altogether. The sea was as calm as water in a bowl. After all the celebrating the night before, everyone was tired, and soon almost the entire crew was fast asleep.

Around midnight, even the Admiral lay down to get some sleep. Everything was calm and quiet. With the sea so calm, what could go wrong? We soon found out.

Some time after midnight we were awakened by shouts. It was Juan de la Cosa, the ship's owner. What was he saying?

We had run aground! Though there was no wind, a strong current had carried the *Santa María* onto a reef.

At first there was so much excitement, no one knew what had happened. The Admiral ordered Juan de la Cosa to get into the small batel and cast our anchor at the stern, to stop our drift onto the reef. De la Cosa and some seamen jumped into the batel. But they made no move to cast the anchor. Instead, they rowed with haste to the *Niña*.

We were astonished. Juan de la Cosa is the owner of the *Santa María*. You would think he would do all he could to save it. But his only thought was to save his own neck, and forget about the rest of us—and his ship.

The Admiral then ordered that the mainmast be cut down and thrown overboard. This would lighten our weight, maybe enough to allow us to drift off the reef. But it didn't work. The ship listed more and more to the side. Then the seams opened, and water began pouring into the hold.

The Admiral shouted, "Abandon ship!" Luis and I looked at each other, then jumped. We

swam to the *Niña* and climbed aboard. The Admiral was the last to leave the *Santa María*. He stood on the sloping deck, holding his log book, and waited for the batel to pick him up.

It was not till we reached the *Niña* that we found out how the accident happened. Around midnight, with everyone asleep and the sea as calm as water in a tub, the helmsman decided to go to sleep, too. Was no one at the tiller when we hit? Yes, he left the tiller in the control of one of the few people who were still awake. Someone who had no experience as a helmsman, and did not sense the ship's drift. Who was it? That was the one thing we did not know.

There was no way now we could save the poor old *Santa María*. But we could try to salvage our supplies. The Admiral sent Diego de Arana to find the Cacique Guacanagari to see if he and his people could help us.

Soon, many *canoa*s arrived. The Cacique himself helped with the unloading.

Back on the *Santa María*, I looked around for my bag. It had slid to the rail. I pulled out my book and stuck it in my shirt.

With the swift help of the Indians, we managed to save everything—our stores, our casks, our navigational equipment, our spare ampolletas, our maps and charts.

Not only did the Cacique Guacanagari help us unload. He had his men empty some houses, so we could store our things there.

I cannot get over these people. They are affectionate. They seem free of greed. They are gentle, and always smiling. They obey their Cacique without question. And they are so generous.

When every last thing was saved, we threw ourselves down to sleep.

What a Christmas!

When Luis, Manuel, and I awoke, we saw a strange sight. The Admiral was shouting at Juan de la Cosa and a seaman. Standing beside them was Diego. His face was white. He looked scared.

What was going on?

We edged closer.

The Admiral was speaking now to de la Cosa and to the seaman. "I don't blame the boy. I blame you. How many times have I said that no gromet should ever be in control of the tiller!"

Luis, Manuel, and I looked at each other. It was Diego who was at the tiller when the *Santa María* went aground.

Soon the group split up. Diego ran off into the woods. We followed, and found him sitting weeping under a palm tree. We tried to console him.

"It could have happened no matter *who* was at the tiller," said Manuel.

"You heard the Admiral. It's not your fault," I added.

Diego paid no attention to us.

Diego, who was so eager to be a good seaman . . .

He refused to come back with us. We left him sitting there alone.

Now, a terrible question arose in my mind. With the *Santa María* wrecked, how would we ever get home?

True to his nature, the Admiral saw no problem. He had not been discouraged when our journey here took so long. Nor when we kept failing to find the source of gold. Or the Court of the Great Khan. And now he was not even discouraged by the wrecking of the *Santa María*! As usual he had hope. And he soon had an answer to everything.

At sunset, we all gathered on the deck of the *Niña*. After the usual evening prayers, this is what he told us:

"I see now," he said, "that everything was the will of God. The disaster was really a blessing in disguise. I recognize that our Lord has caused us to run aground at this place so that we might establish a settlement here. I have thought of the name for the settlement. It is to be called Villa de la Navidad [Christmas town]."

He went on to tell us his plan. A tower and a fortress will be built here. And a group of our good men will remain. Diego de Arana will be in charge. Second in command will be Pedro Gutiérrez. And to assist, Rodrigo de Escobedo will remain. The rest of us will return to Spain on the *Niña*. Manuel gave me a poke in the ribs. Pepe sighed with relief.

The Admiral went on. "To construct the fortress, you can use the timber from the *Santa María*. I will leave enough biscuits and wine for more than a year. I will leave seeds for sowing, and also the ship's batel. . . . I truly believe that everything that has happened was for this purpose; that this beginning may be made. I hope to God that when I come back here from Spain, which I intend to do very soon, our settlers will have discovered the gold mine, and I will find a barrel of gold waiting here."

Then he called for volunteers.

One by one, men stepped up. Francisco, a caulker. Antonio, a gunner. Domingo, a cask maker. Then a physician. A carpenter. A tailor. Soon thirty-eight men—most from the *Santa María,* but also some from the *Niña*—stood there. Then Diego stepped forward. Diego—whose heart's desire was to be a sailor. Not a settler in this far-off land.

Luis and I looked at each other. We knew why he was doing it. It was to punish himself—for the sinking of the *Santa María.*

Later we tried to convince him that this was the wrong thing for him to do. That he should come back and be a seaman. But he just shook his head and would not even talk about it.

27 December. An Indian messenger has reported to Cacique Guacanagari that he has seen the *Pinta*! It was in a harbor at the far end of the island. Whether the *Pinta* joins us in time or not, the Admiral still plans to return to Spain as soon as possible.

Good-bye to
the Cacique

30 December. During the past few days, there have been many farewell parties. Today all hands were given a feast by the Cacique. We ate shrimp, and fowl, and caçabi, and fruit, and game. Pepe remarked that this is probably the first and last time we (the gromets) would ever be entertained by a king.

Today the Cacique put a gold crown on the Admiral's head. The Admiral then presented the Cacique with a beautiful necklace of blood-stones, and a scarlet cloak, and a silver ring, and a pair of gloves. Can you believe this? The Cacique is most interested in the gloves! I guess he has never seen gloves. They don't need them here.

31 December. We spent the entire day loading water and wood and food on board the *Niña* for our return voyage.

Leaving La
Navidad

2 January 1493. The Admiral said his last good-byes to his friend Guacanagari. Then he gathered together all the men who are to remain at La Navidad. He asked that they obey their leader, Diego de Arana, and that they respect Cacique Guacanagari. He asked that they never annoy the Indians, reminding them how much we all owe these people.

Last, he promised that he will ask Queen Isabella and King Ferdinand for special rewards for the men of La Navidad, which he, the Admiral, will give out when he returns.

He is right. How kind these people have been to us. Nothing like those fierce dog-faced Canibales we heard about!

4 January. As the sun rises, we pull up our anchors and set sail for home. As we leave the harbor, we see a small figure, who has climbed to the top of a palm tree and is waving a shirt at us.

It is Diego. Poor Diego . . .

Part III

The Voyage Home

5 January.   The plan is to sail east, hugging the north coast of La Isla Española. How big is this island anyhow? We will find out.

How big is La Isla Española?

The little *Niña* is crowded. It now carries most of its own crew, plus extras (us) from the *Santa María*. Plus a lot of Indians! Still, the crew is in good spirits, because 1. We are going home, and 2. Everyone has great faith in the Admiral now.

6 January.   What a welcome sight! The lookout in the crow's nest has spotted the *Pinta* approaching! They draw alongside and Captain Martin Pinzón comes aboard. He apologizes to the Admiral and gives at least a dozen reasons why he sailed off on his own, and why he did not return sooner: . . . they were becalmed . . . the wind was too strong . . . they ran out of

105

food . . . he had this trouble and that. . . . I can see by the Admiral's face that he doesn't believe a word of it. Still, it is a good thing they have joined us. It is safer for two ships to sail on the open seas than one alone.

By the way, he found no gold at Babeque.

7 January. The *Niña* is leaking. We pump out the bilge, and fill in the seams to make her watertight. Better to do this now than later, when out in open sea.

Gold! | **8 January.** How strange. Now that we are not looking for it, we have found gold! This is how it happened. We went up a river to get some fresh water. Then we noticed the barrel hoops were glittering. Small bits of gold were stuck in them! The sand hereabouts is filled with gold. But only small pieces. They are about the size of little seeds. Probably there is a gold mine far up the river. We will not try to find it now. But you can be sure the Admiral has marked this spot very carefully on his map. He named the river El Río del Oro [River of Gold].

12 January. We continue to sail east along the north coast of La Isla Española, passing mountains and capes, all of which the Admiral names: Silver Mountain . . . Angel Cape . . . Iron Cape . . . Round Cape . . . Cape of Good Weather . . . Cape of the Flaked Rock. *Giant tortoises*

There are, in this land, many big tortoises. They look like big wooden shields. These giant creatures come onshore to lay their eggs, which they bury in the sand. Today some of the men brought back hats full of eggs. A nice change in diet.

Tonight, at sunset, I saw three big ugly whiskered creatures sitting on a rock. The sailors call them "sirena." Two of the Indians aboard pointed to them and called out, "Manati!" I guess that is the Indian name for them.

I make sure to mention all the wild creatures I see. Brother Gustavo will be interested in this, I know. Just think. Soon I will see him.

13 January. Today we sailed into a large bay. To the east there are high white cliffs. On seeing them, the Admiral said, "Let us call this place Cabo del Enamorado [Lover's Cape]." *Lover's Cape*

107

Luis de Torres nodded and said, "A good name." I thought it was an odd name, till Manuel explained it to me. It seems that these cliffs look like cliffs that have that name near the city of Granada.

Since Gutiérrez, Escobedo, and Rodrigo de Arana all remained at Navidad, the Admiral spends a lot of time now with Señor de Torres. Juan de la Cosa is also aboard. But since his cowardly deserting of the sinking *Santa María*, the Admiral does not even talk to him.

We anchored here. Onshore, some of our men met up with charcoal-smeared Indians wearing headbands made of parrot feathers. Our men wanted to trade with them. But a fight soon broke out.

One of our men slashed an Indian in the rear end. The others all picked up their bows and arrows and ran off.

Is this the Canibale tribe that is supposed to eat men? Nobody waited to find out.

Luis showed me a spear he brought back. It had a fishbone at the end, and poison on the tip.

16 January. Bad news. The *Niña* and the *Pinta* are both leaking badly. Can we cross the ocean this way?

At evening prayers, the Admiral said, "I have faith in our Lord, who brought us here and who will lead us back in his pity and mercy. . . . Almighty God will take care of everything."

Some of the men looked doubtful.

The Admiral named this place Golfo de las Flechas [Gulf of Arrows].

We remained here several days because the wind was contrary and the bay very rough. But last night the wind changed. Three hours before dawn, we set sail. We are now on the open sea.

18 January. The breeze has been mild. But we are making steady headway. We have covered about two hundred miles since leaving La Isla Española. "At this rate," I tell Pepe, "we will be home in little over a month." We see big frigate birds flying overhead, and many smaller birds as well.

Yesterday we began to see tuna fish. Today the sea is clogged with them. The men tried to spear some, but failed. Too bad, because we have nothing left to eat but caçabi bread, wine, and water. Later on, the men managed to spear a large shark. I helped Francisco cut it up and put it in the cookpot. A welcome change from bread and water.

The Indians | **22 January.** Dead calm today. As we sit here in the quiet water, the Indians go swimming. They do not like washing in buckets, the way we do on board. They are enjoying their swim.

Of all the Indians taken on board, there are now only six left. All the rest have died.

At first I was making friends with the Indians, especially the five young men, who were just a bit older than I. I taught them some of our words. They taught me some of theirs. But now those who are left have practically stopped talking, even to each other. They have no spirit left.

They eat very little. And they are very uneasy about relieving themselves the way we have to on board—sitting on those seats, over the sea, that are attached to the stern. (We don't like that either. But it is the way it has to be.)

Now Luis and I watched them swim, and even thought of joining them. They looked almost

110

happy in the water.

"I think they are all dying of heartbreak," Luis said. Luis and I often think the same things. I guess that is why we have become such good friends.

23 January. As we sail northeast, the breeze is cooler and the nights longer. The wind has become strong and changeable. Several times Manuel, Pepe, Luis, and I are asked to help control the sails. I can see the voyage home is going to be much rougher sailing than our voyage *to* the Indies. Coming over, we had the wind behind us from the east. With the wind pushing us from behind, and the sails let out as far as they could go, the ships practically flew over the water. We are now going against the wind. A ship cannot sail straight into the wind. Instead, we must tack. This means taking a zigzag course, always at an angle to the wind. Sailing this way, close to the wind, is much harder.

The *Pinta* is having trouble. The mainmast is weak. Sailing close-hauled puts a strain on it. Several times we have had to wait for her to catch up.

2 February. Thanks be to God. For several days the breeze has been gentle and the sea calm. We are coming into patches of seaweed. We are not worried about it, as we were on our passage over. We move through it steadily at a speed of five knots. In the past eleven hours, we have gone fifty-seven miles.

Today's sightings:

    20 white-headed terns
    7 long-winged petrels
    1 huge frigate bird, diving for fish
    7 blue dorado fish, 6 feet long, swimming
        close to the ship
    Porpoises: too many to count

3 February. I am on duty for the late shift, from three to seven in the morning. We are sailing at a speed of seven or eight knots, sometimes nine. Through the night we cover ninety-seven miles. It is raining and cold. My throat hurts. I am just barely able to sing my ditties.

Homeward bound, Luis and I have many conversations about what we are going to do when we get home. We both want to grow things. I favor fruit trees. Luis prefers vegetables. (He still has that *ajes* plant, wrapped in a leaf. It doesn't look so good. But he is confident it will revive! That's the way he is, Luis—always sure the best will happen.)

As the voyage progresses, so do our ideas. And soon we have a very special plan.

6 February. Our best day yet! Through the night, according to the Admiral, we sailed 107 miles. During the day, we ran at a speed of 10 knots, and covered another 115 miles. 222 miles in 24 hours! Luis and I exchange glances during the change of the watch. At this rate, we will be home in no time!

10 February. They just finished a big meeting up on the poop deck. Captain Vincente Pinzón; Peralonso and Bartolomé, the two pilots of the *Niña*; Sancho Ruiz, who was the pilot of the *Santa María*; and of course the Admiral. With all these experts, it seems nobody can agree exactly where we are. The pilots think we are closer to Spain than does the Admiral.

I hope the pilots are right.

A good breeze is pushing us along. Everyone is cheerful.

The storm | **13 February.** It was all too good to be true. The weather has changed. The waves are high. The wind is coming in short bursts from every which way. The Admiral has ordered us to pull down the sails altogether. That way, a sudden gust will be less likely to make us capsize. Now there is no separation between gromet and seaman. We all have to help. There are flashes of lightning.

14 February. Last night the wind got stronger. Huge waves came at us from both directions and broke over the deck. We could feel the *Niña* tremble as waves pounded it from both sides. The Admiral ordered that we run before the wind. This means we do not even try to guide the ship, but let the wind push us where it will. We hunkered down with our arms around each other, to anchor ourselves down. Also, to give each other courage.

Could things get any worse? Yes. During the night, the *Pinta* disappeared from sight.

114

Around me I hear the men mumbling and praying. We all have cramps in our legs from the wet and the cold. No one has slept for days. No one expects to survive.

Today at dusk there was a slight lull. The Admiral shouted into the wind, "Men. Listen to me. I believe God will help us fulfill what we have begun. I know He will deliver us safely. . . ." The Admiral asked us to vow then and there that when we do reach land, the first thing we will do will be to go in a procession to church and pray.

Despite his words, I think that even the Admiral now feels that our luck may have run out. Here is what makes me think so. Yesterday his servant, Salcedo, told me what the Admiral has been doing. He has been busy writing, on a piece of parchment, about all we have done, and the lands we have claimed, and about La Navidad, and where it is. When finished, he put the parchment in a waxed cloth, tied it tight, placed it in a barrel, and had Salcedo throw it into the sea.

It is clear: He thinks there is a chance we may go down. If we do, it is his hope that someone might find the barrel and deliver the document to

Queen Isabella and King Ferdinand, so that they will know that we *did* succeed, and did reach the Indies and claim many lands for them.

I carry my own book tucked into my shirt. It is very waterlogged and hard to write in.

Through the night, Luis and I hang on to each other on the shifting deck. We had such great plans for the future. Now we just wonder whether we will live to see another day.

The Azore Islands | **15 February.** Are we imagining things? As the sun rises, we see land. The Admiral was right again. God *is* watching over us. We have reached the island of Santa María, one of the Azore Islands.

19 February. After all we have been through, what happened today is almost a joke! Half of the crew went ashore, Luis and Manuel among them. True to the vow we had taken, they went, first thing, to a church to pray. While praying, they were seized by the villagers and thrown in jail.

We waited, but they did not come back. Then the Admiral met with Captain João de

Castanheira, ruler of this island, who told him our men were in jail.

Why? Because, replied the Captain, he thinks we have been to West Africa, which is not permitted, since that part of the world belongs to Portugal.

The Admiral stated that we have not been to Africa. Furthermore, he is the Admiral of the Ocean Sea, and Viceroy of the Indies, representing the King and Queen of Spain, and he demands the release of our men at once.

The stubborn Captain replied that the Azores are part of Portugal, and he therefore does not recognize the wishes of the rulers of Spain. He then left.

What now? I hate to think of Luis and Manuel in jail.

22 February. The Admiral has finally convinced the Captain that we have not been to West Africa. After much talk back and forth, he agrees to release our men. Soon they appear in the boat. We reach down to help them back on board. The rest of us will certainly not fulfill our vows in this place! We will set sail tomorrow.

4 March. For more than a week the sea has been calm. We sailed steadily toward home. Then the wind shifted. Suddenly, last night, a fierce squall blew up, ripping our sails to shreds. We moved ahead with bare masts, and hung on to anything we could, as the *Niña* pitched back and forth, the huge waves slapping it first from one side, then the other. The wind was so strong that at times it seemed to lift our ship up into the air.

There was a full moon. Suddenly we saw signs of land. How often we had wished for just that sight. But not like this. Because dead ahead, not five miles away, we spied high rocky cliffs.

How could we avoid them? Had we come this far only to smash up so close to home? It seemed only a miracle could save us.

We had one small extra sail saved in a locker. Hoisting this with great difficulty, we managed to change direction and avoid the cliffs.

When the sun came up, we could see where we were. The Rock of Sintra, near Lisbon, Portugal. We entered the Tagus river and in a few hours were safely anchored.

We are safe.

We are alive.

Then, in the midst of our rejoicing, we began to wonder: What has happened to the *Pinta*?

As soon as we anchored, the Admiral sent a letter to King John II of Portugal, asking permission to proceed up the river to Lisbon, where we could refit our ship with new sails. After our strange reception in the Azores, he is a bit worried. Are Portugal and Spain now on bad terms? We have been away so long, we don't know. The Admiral waits for his answer.

8 March.   The King of Portugal has answered the Admiral. His letter is very friendly. We may, he says, proceed to Lisbon, where the *Niña* is to be supplied with everything that we need. And he, the King, will pay for it. He also invites the Admiral to visit him at Valle de Paraíso, twenty-seven miles from Lisbon, where he is now staying. He wishes, he writes, to learn all about our voyage.

The royal invitation

★ ★ ★

I heard the Admiral and Vincente Pinzón talking this over. The Admiral is not eager to go. Instead, he wishes to report with all speed directly to Queen Isabella and King Ferdinand. He fears they will be angry if another ruler learns of our discoveries before they do. But how can he refuse this invitation, when King John has been so kind? And Pinzón shrewdly points out to him, "Sometimes an invitation is more like an order."

The Admiral has decided to go, and take along three of the Indians, to prove to King John that we have truly reached the Indies. And since I have spent more time with the Indians than most, he has asked me to come along!

King John of Portugal | **9 March.** We set off along muddy roads, on mule back, the trip taking more than a day. At last we reached the place where the King was staying—a monastery called Santa María das Virtudes. There the Admiral was received with great courtesy. He spent hours telling King John all we had seen. The King was most interested— especially in the Indians, because they looked like

120

no people he had ever seen before. He watched as they made an outline of their islands, using beans. Over their heads, King John nodded at the Admiral. Then he did a very unkinglike thing. He smacked himself on the chest, saying, "Why did I let slip such a wonderful chance?"

It was hard for me to keep back a smile when this happened. We all know, by now, that the Admiral had first asked King John (who was then Prince John) to sponsor his voyage. But John refused. Now he is sorry. For all these lands we discovered now belong to Spain, and not to Portugal.

We made one more stop, to a nearby convent where the Queen was staying. The Admiral paid his respects. Then, at last, we were free to return.

The plan | **12 March.** While we were gone, the *Niña* has been fitted with new sails and lines. Food, water, and wine have been loaded aboard. She is ready to sail home to Spain.

I have never seen the Admiral so cheerful. And why not? He has done something no one has ever done before—reached the Indies by sailing west, across an unknown ocean. People had laughed at him. They called him a clown. And a fool. Now he has proved himself right . . . and all of them wrong. Now he can laugh at them! No wonder he is cheerful.

Even now, he is planning a return voyage to the Indies. He hopes to leave in less than a year. He is getting a crew ready. And he has asked *me* to go on the next voyage!

I was honored, but I said no. I told him why. The voyage was thrilling. I will never forget it. And I will always be glad that I came along. But I know now what I really want to do. I want to grow things—oranges and lemons, almonds and apricots. I can see it all in my mind, with all the colors on the hillside. And I want to raise canaries.

Pepe is happy thinking about going home to be a bootmaker. Manuel has said yes to the Admiral's invitation and signed on to return to the Indies. We look at each other and think about Diego. "I will try and get him to come back with me," Manuel tells us.

And Luis? At last we tell our friends about our plan. We are going to be farmers—together.

On the voyage, we have each earned three thousand maravedies. Luis sent one thousand of his to his mother with Pepe. So, with my three thousand and Luis's two thousand, we have five thousand maravedies. Is that enough to buy land? Maybe a small piece? We are not sure.

Well, Brother Gustavo can help and advise us. He has taught me almost everything else I know. Why should he stop now?

For a time, we can live at the friary. I know the Brothers will take Luis to their hearts, as they did me. I am smiling now—thinking about the thousand questions they will ask us.

This may all seem dull to the Admiral. But to me, it seems wonderful.

13 March. At eight o'clock this morning, the *Niña* set sail for Seville. Luis and I remain in Lisbon, where we hope to sign onto a ship that will take us to the Canary Islands.

Now the third part of my life is beginning. God willing, it will be a good one.

Signed,

Julio de la Vega Medina
This day of our Lord
13 March 1493

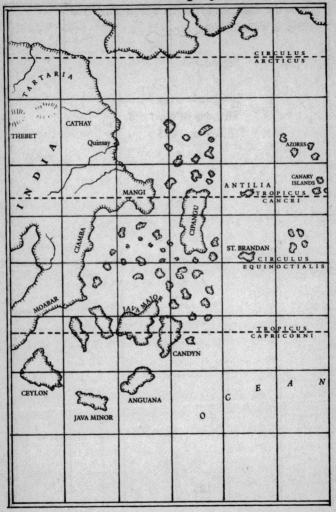

CIRCULUS
ARCTICUS

TARTARIA

THEBET   CATHAY

Quinsay

AZORES

INDIA

CANARY
ISLANDS

ANTILIA

MANGI   TROPICUS
CANCRI

CIAMBA   CIPANGU

ST. BRANDAN

CIRCULUS
EQUINOCTIALIS

MOABAR   JAVA MAJOR

TROPICUS
CAPRICORNI

CANDYN

O   C   E   A   N

CEYLON   ANGUANA   C

O

JAVA MINOR

World in 1492

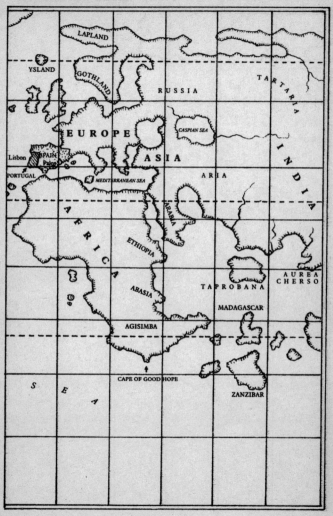

Author's Note

This book is not a real diary. But it could have been. In this book, only the characters of Julio and the other gromets are made up. Everything else is based on historical fact. The events of each day are based on Columbus's written log. The names of all the other characters—Pedro Gutiérrez, Juan de la Cosa, Diego de Arana, Rodrigo de Escobedo, Luis de Torres, Martin and Vincente Pinzón, the pilots Ruiz and Peralonso—are all true names of people who went on the voyage.

It is true that Columbus gave false lower mileage figures to his crew. He did this because he felt the men would be less frightened if they thought they had traveled less far from home. The fact is, Columbus mistakenly overestimated the speed at which they were sailing. So in reality they were not sailing as far each day as he thought. Oddly enough, this means that the "false" figures he gave out to the crew each day turned out to be more accurate than what he thought were the true figures.

On page 22 the officers talk about a journey of

2,400 miles. The scientific opinion of the time was that the distance between the Canary Islands and Cipangu was more like 3,000 miles. Columbus gave out a lower figure because he had honestly miscalculated the size of the earth and thought it was smaller than it is. He also deliberately said that the voyage would be shorter than he actually thought, so that it would not seem as difficult, and this would make it easier for him to get financial backing. (The real distance from the Canary Islands to Japan [Cipangu] is more like 10,000 miles.)

Antilia was supposedly an island somewhere west of the Canary Islands. It was placed on maps of the time. The truth is there is no such island.

The weeds the ships went through are in an area of the Atlantic Ocean called the Sargasso Sea, which still exists, and covers an area of about 2 million square miles.

The weeds in it originally tore loose from land, and adapted to being able to live and grow in the sea. Crabs, shrimps, fish, and barnacles can live among these weeds. The native people encountered were members of the Arawak tribes.

Some of their words we now use:

hamaca = hammock

canoa = canoe

manati = manatee, a sea mammal also called a
sea cow

From the tribes called Canibales (who sometimes did eat human flesh) we get the word can-
nibal. The Canibales were sometimes called
Caribes, or Caribs. From this we get the word
Caribbean.

The edible root they called *ajes* is what we call
manioc, or cassava.

Some experts think that Columbus's first landing place—San Salvador—was an island in the
Bahamas that was later called Watlings Island.
Recently the name of this island has been offi-
cially changed back to Columbus's original name
for it—San Salvador. Other experts think the first
landing place was a different island now called
Samana Cay. There are five or six additional islands that are also possibilities.

The island Columbus named Santa María de
la Concepción is now called Rum Cay.

Fernandina is now called Long Island.

Isabela is now called Crooked Island.

(ATLANTIC OCEAN)

(FLORIDA)

BAHAMAS

CUBA

WATLINGS ISLAND
(San Salvador)

RUM CAY
(Santa María de la Concepción)

LONG ISLAND
(Fernandina)

SAMANA CAY

CROOKED ISLAND
(Isabela)

GRAND INAGUA
(Babeque)

ÎLE DE LA TORTUE
(Isla de la Tortuga)

La Navidad

Valle del Paraiso

Río del Oro

HISPANIOLA
(La Isla Española)

Cabo del Enamorado

Golfo de las Flechas

THE NEW WORLD

The island Columbus named Juana is now Cuba.

Tortuga is now called Ile de la Tortue (the French name meaning Tortoise Island).

La Isla Española (sometimes called Hispaniola) is the island now shared by Haiti and the Dominican Republic.

Babeque is now called Grand Inagua Island.

There is a lot of mystery surrounding the life of Columbus. It is thought that he was born in Genoa, Italy. No one is absolutely sure about the year he was born. Most say it was 1451. But some say it was 1460; others say 1435. He spoke Spanish fluently but with a slight accent. (This is why the sailors called him "the foreigner.")

Columbus made four voyages in all to "the Indies." On the second voyage, made in 1493, he headed first for La Navidad. Arriving there in November, he discovered that every single settler was dead. Evidently, disobeying Columbus's final orders, they had roamed over the island, fought with the Indians, and finally were killed by them.

Till the day he died, Columbus was certain that he had reached the Indies. At the time, just about everyone agreed with him. (Only one man, an Italian named Peter Martyr d'Anghieri, insisted that the size of the earth showed that Columbus could not possibly have reached the Indies, and that he must have discovered "a new world.") It was not until the year 1510 that some others began to think that perhaps a new land had been found, and that Columbus had not reached the Indies after all.

Columbus died in Valladolid, Spain, on May 20, 1506.

Finally, what did happen to the *Pinta*?

On March 15, 1493, Columbus, on the *Niña*, reached Palos, Spain, the original starting place he had left 224 days before. The *Pinta* arrived there the very same day! (By traveling on a northern route, the *Pinta* had missed the big storms that the *Niña* had encountered.)

Rodrigo de Triana, the seaman who first sighted land, never received his reward. Since Columbus reported that he himself had seen a light the night before, Queen Isabella ruled that Columbus had really been the first to sight land, and therefore de Triana was not entitled to the reward.